TRICK
YOUR WHEELS,
TUNE YOUR RIDE
By Heather Dakota
P9-DGH-423
67
1

Written by Heather Dakota
Illustrated and designed by Deena Fleming

All rights reserved. No part of this publication may be reproduced, or stored in a retrieval system, or transmitted in any form or by any means, electronic, mechanical, photocopying, recording, or otherwise, without written permission of
Tangerine Press.

Copyright© 2005 Scholastic Inc

Scholastic and Tangerine Press and associated logos are trademarks of Scholastic Inc

Published by Tangerine Press, an imprint of
Scholastic Inc; 557 Broadway; New York, NY 10012

10 9 8 7 6 5 4 3 2 1

ISBN 0-439-83287-X

Printed and bound in China
photographs p.61 ©Heelys
photographs p. 47-49 ©Keith Jacobs
photograph p. 59 ©Mark Maziarz

Heelys logo is a trademark of HSL, used with permission.
Bicycles and bike equipment courtesy of
Lake Mary Cycles.

Scholastic Canada
Markham, Ontario
Scholastic Australia
Gosford, NSW
Scholastic New Zealand
Greenmount, Auckland

an imprint of
SCHOLASTIC
www.scholastic.com

TABLE OF CONTENTS

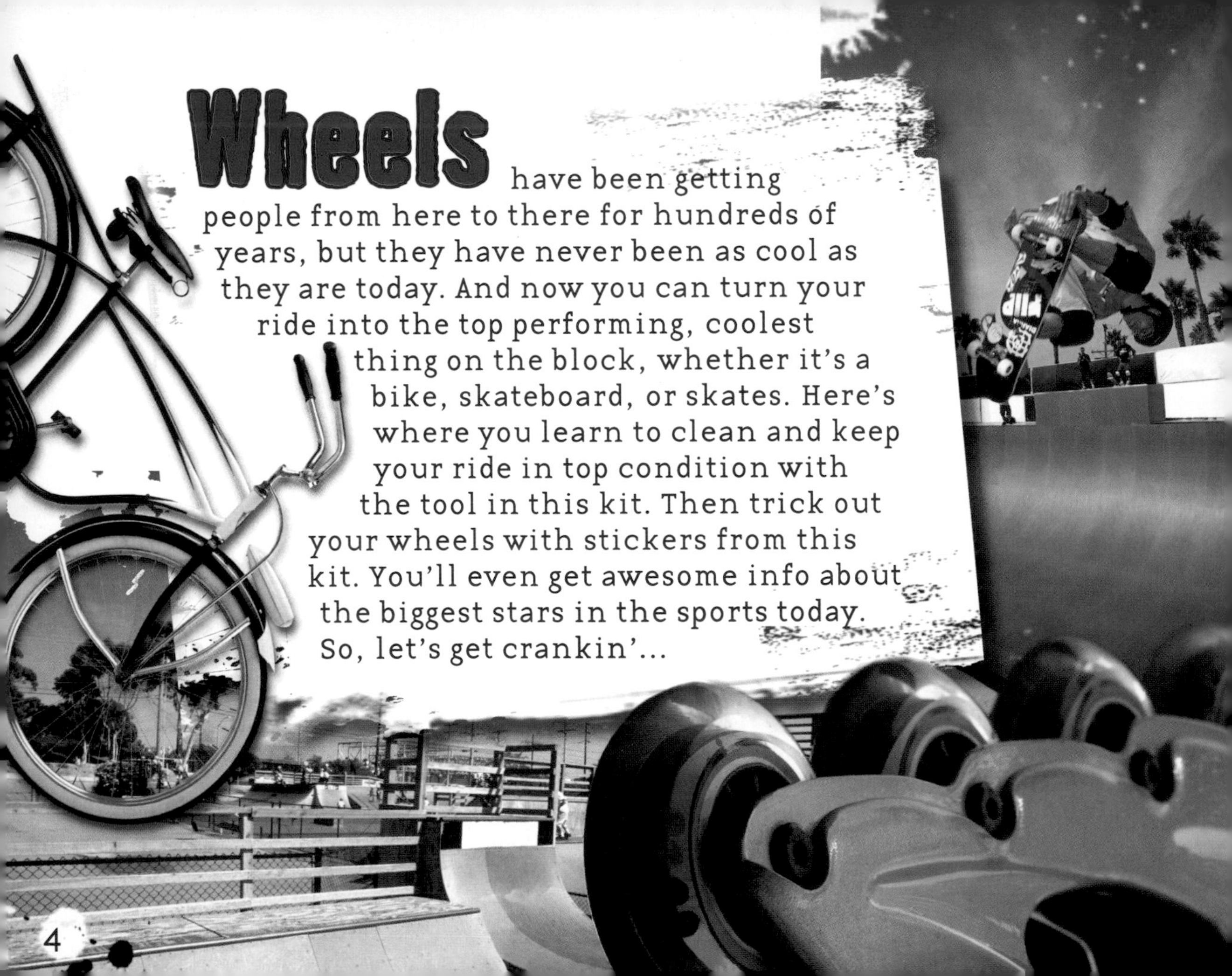

Wheels have been getting people from here to there for hundreds of years, but they have never been as cool as they are today. And now you can turn your ride into the top performing, coolest thing on the block, whether it's a bike, skateboard, or skates. Here's where you learn to clean and keep your ride in top condition with the tool in this kit. Then trick out your wheels with stickers from this kit. You'll even get awesome info about the biggest stars in the sports today. So, let's get crankin'...

Your included all purpose tool

PHILLIPS HEAD SCREWDRIVER

FLATHEAD SCREWDRIVER

5MM ALLEN WRENCH

1MM ALLEN WRENCH

Tune Your Ride

6MM ALLEN WRENCH

15MM BOX WRENCH

8MM BOX WRENCH

THE BIKE

A little background check...

Here's the skinny on the bicycle. Some form or another of a bike has been around since the 1400s. Leonardo Da Vinci sketched a primitive type of bike in his journals. The "hobby horse" came along in the 18th century, but there weren't any peddles yet. (Can you imagine?) All the basic elements of the modern bicycle were brought together in the Starley 1885 "Rover." Improvements after that were slow going. It's only been in the last 20 years or so that there have been advances in the materials used, an increase in gears, and an improvement in wheel design. (Lucky you!)

Melissa Sanborn

Bikes are not just for boys! Melissa Sanborn started in sports at age 12. She played tennis and soccer throughout high school and college. Melissa started cycling in the summer of 1999 when she purchased a racing bike. And the rest is history! She competed in the 2004 Olympic games and has numerous first place wins.

Use Your Head!

Safety first in all things, and biking is no exception. Here's what you need to stay safe:

Dude, wearing a helmet is not an option if you value your life! And it must fit right if it's going to do its job. Any bike store can help you find a helmet to fit your head. As a general rule, a helmet should:

- *Sit level and firm on your head and not tilt forward, backward, or sideways*
- *Have strong, wide straps that fasten under your chin with no more than a finger's width underneath the strap*
- *Be tight enough (with straps fastened) that when you pull or twist, the helmet does not move around on your head*
- *Never be worn over any other head gear*
- *If you take a serious hit, fall, or if the helmet comes into contact with any hard surface, it needs to be replaced immediately.*

mountain biking:

*Hydration backpack

*Eye protection (can be sports sunglasses)

*Gloves

*Padded mountain bike shorts

*Mountain bike shoes (they have special cleats that fit your pedal)

RACING:

*Helmet

*Bike Shorts

*Shoes (either that fit into pedal grips or that are cleated to fit your pedal)

*Gloves

BMX:

*Shoes– training shoes

*BMX pads– to protect your body from serious injury

*Clothes– long sleeved shirts and pants

*Helmets– racers wear full-face helmets; freestylers wear open-face types with a separate mouth guard. You must wear a helmet in competitions.

*Gloves

What's the best bike for you?

Think about some of these things when you're getting ready to drop some cash on a rad bike! After all, if you don't look and feel fabulous on your new bike, why bother? Remember, bikes are vehicles, not toys. Don't rush into buying one!

ARE YOU GOING TO RIDE YOUR BIKE ON PAVED ROADS, TRAILS, OR A BIKE PARK?

Think about this...If you plan to do serious trail biking, get a mountain bike. You'll need the suspension this type of bike gives you. However, a mountain bike is a heavier bike (to stay on the trail), so if you're going to ride on paved streets, you don't want to be slowed down by the heavy bike. Try a road bike or hybrid for this type of biking. If you plan on jumpin' that ramp, you better have a good BMX bike.

ARE YOU JUST OUT HANGIN' WITH YOUR BUDS, TAKING YOUR SWEET OLD TIME GETTING TO SCHOOL, AND LOOKIN' COOL WHILE YOUR AT IT?

Check out a BMX bike! You'll look great. They get around on paved roads just fine, and you can show off your new street tricks too.

ARE YOU GOING TO RIDE DISTANCES LONGER THAN 10 MILES?

There's no question here, get a bike that is built for riding the pavement! A lightweight frame and smaller gears will help a lot. You can also trade in your stock tires for ones with less tread and more air pressure to breeze on down the road.

DO YOU LIVE IN AN AREA WITH STEEP HILLS?

You'll need a bike that has a lightweight frame and triple crank. The lower gears will make climbing those hills a little easier. It's still a tough ride, but you can do it!

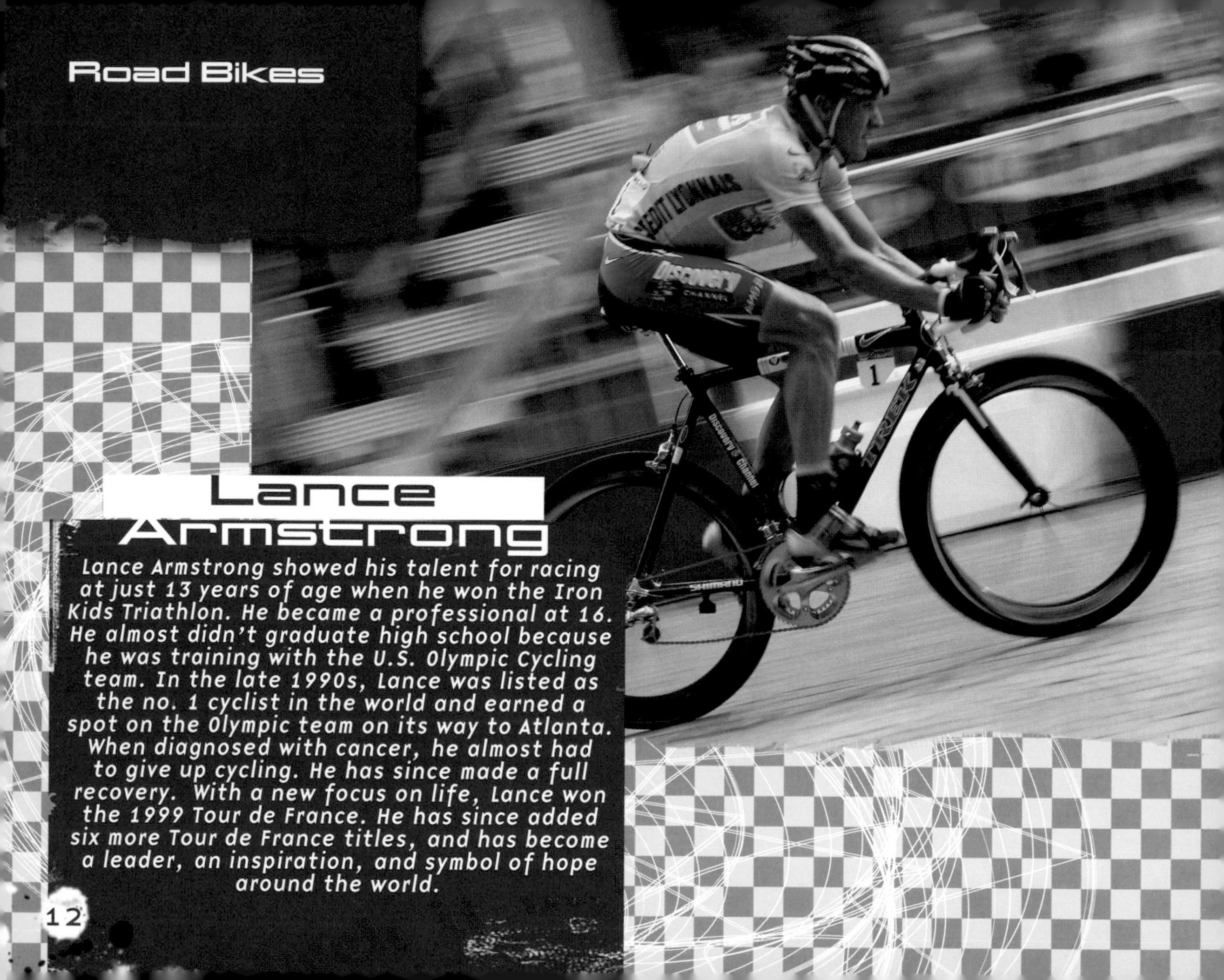

Lance Armstrong

Lance Armstrong showed his talent for racing at just 13 years of age when he won the Iron Kids Triathlon. He became a professional at 16. He almost didn't graduate high school because he was training with the U.S. Olympic Cycling team. In the late 1990s, Lance was listed as the no. 1 cyclist in the world and earned a spot on the Olympic team on its way to Atlanta. When diagnosed with cancer, he almost had to give up cycling. He has since made a full recovery. With a new focus on life, Lance won the 1999 Tour de France. He has since added six more Tour de France titles, and has become a leader, an inspiration, and symbol of hope around the world.

HANDLE BARS
BRAKES
FRAME
PEDALS
TIRES

So you want to try bike racing? Well, pick a local event with a junior race and register. Don't forget you have to have your parent's permission and signature on the form. If this is your first race, you should probably pick a race that has a fairly flat course. It is very discouraging watching a group of riders pull away from you on a climb. And here's the best part—you don't need one of those super fancy bikes to get started. Get a road bike in good condition and you're off!

Tour de France

The Tour de France is one of the world's most famous cycling races. It is a staged race that takes place over three weeks every July since 1903. It started as a way to drum up publicity for the newspaper L'Auto and its rival Paris-Brest et retour. The first winner was Maurice Garin from France. However, American, Lance Armstrong has won the most Tour de France races with six wins. Along with Giro d'Italia (Tour of Italy) and the Vuelta Espana (Tour of Spain), the Tour de France makes up cycling's "Grand Tours."

WHAT'S UP WITH ALL THOSE COLORED JERSEYS?

Riders who lead their class at the end of a stage get to wear a specific colored jersey for the next stage.

Yellow – overall time leader

Green – rider with the most sprint points (awarded depending on the difficulty of the stage and how you place in that stage)

White with Red Polka Dots – King of the Mountain Jersey awarded to the rider who gets to the top of the mountain first

Plain White – awarded to the best overall young rider (under 25 years old)

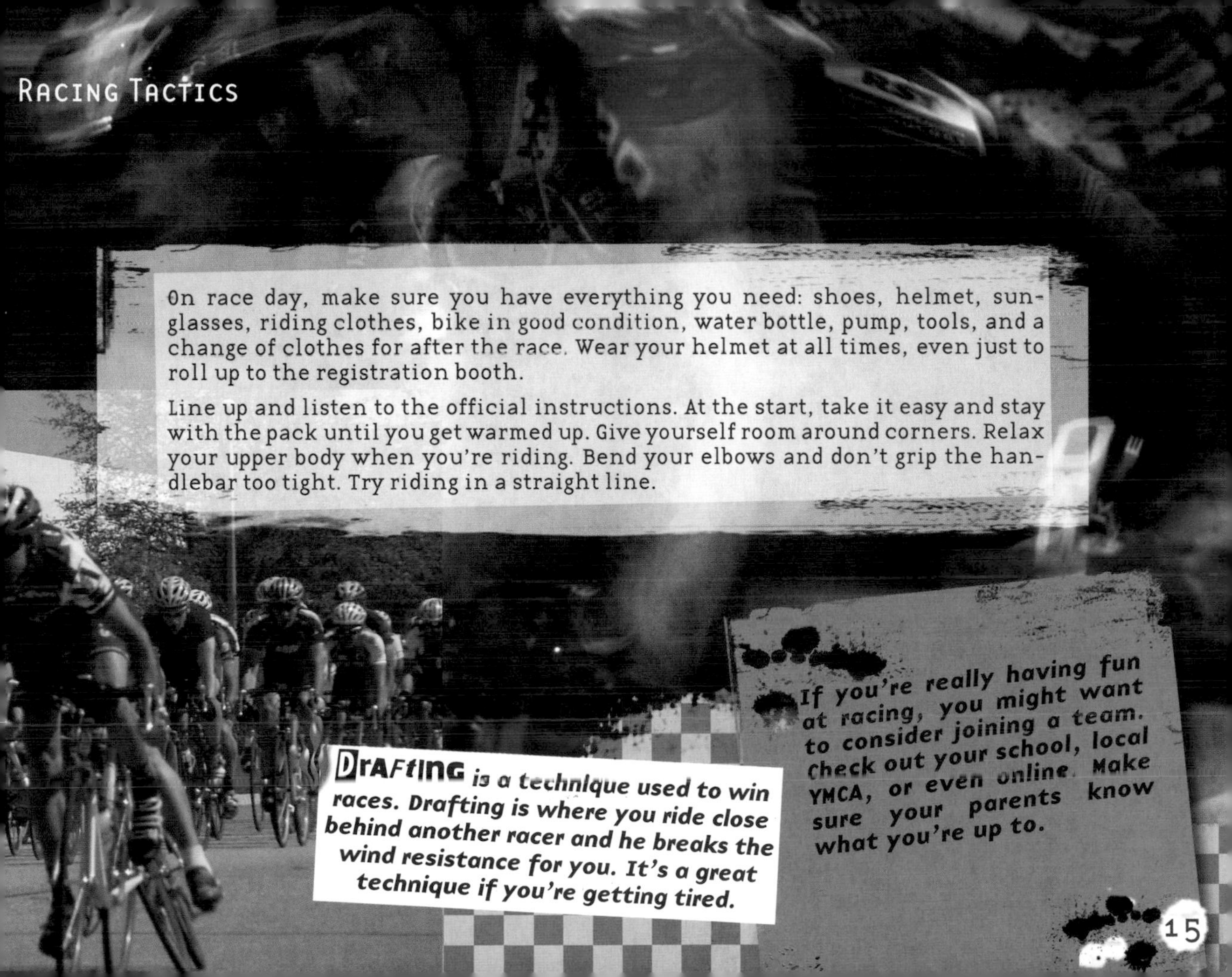

On race day, make sure you have everything you need: shoes, helmet, sunglasses, riding clothes, bike in good condition, water bottle, pump, tools, and a change of clothes for after the race. Wear your helmet at all times, even just to roll up to the registration booth.

Line up and listen to the official instructions. At the start, take it easy and stay with the pack until you get warmed up. Give yourself room around corners. Relax your upper body when you're riding. Bend your elbows and don't grip the handlebar too tight. Try riding in a straight line.

Drafting is a technique used to win races. Drafting is where you ride close behind another racer and he breaks the wind resistance for you. It's a great technique if you're getting tired.

If you're really having fun at racing, you might want to consider joining a team. Check out your school, local YMCA, or even online. Make sure your parents know what you're up to.

History

In 1963, Schwinn introduced the "Sting-Ray." This was the bike that launched the BMX craze. BMX or bicycle motocross started in the 1970s in California, USA. Kids wanted to get the same excitement they were watching with actual motocross. They started making their own ramps and developing new tricks. BMX racing led to the formation of the American Bicycle Association, and they're still organizing races now.

Dave Mirra got hooked on BMX when he was very young. He would get together with friends and jump curbs and build ramps, anything to get some big air. At 13 years old, Dave started getting some national attention for his flatland tricks, but in the late 80s, he started catching some big air in vert events and was hooked. At age 18, Dave broke Mat Hoffman's three-year winning streak. Dave still rides all the time!

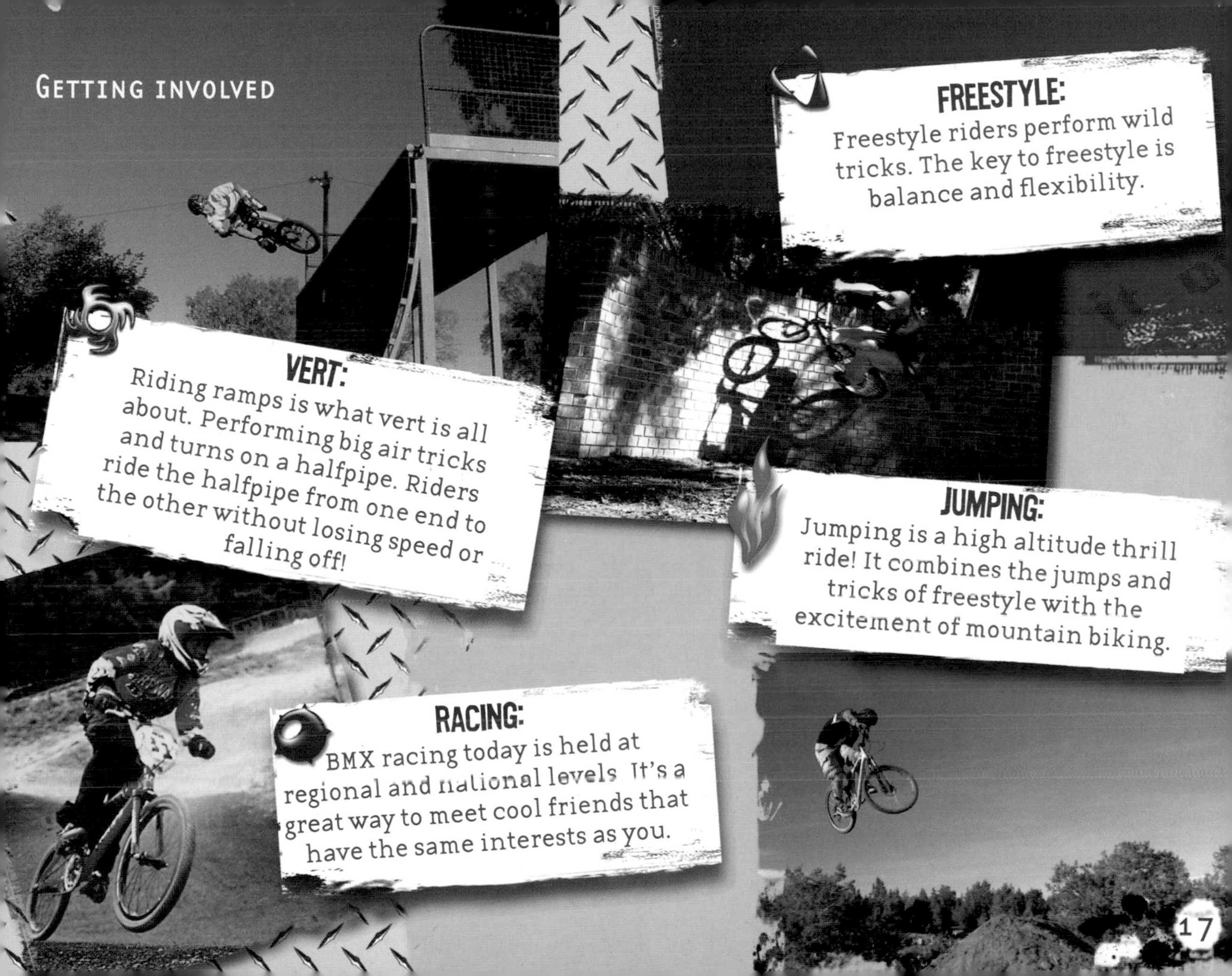

FREESTYLE:

Freestyle riders perform wild tricks. The key to freestyle is balance and flexibility.

VERT:

Riding ramps is what vert is all about. Performing big air tricks and turns on a halfpipe. Riders ride the halfpipe from one end to the other without losing speed or falling off!

JUMPING:

Jumping is a high altitude thrill ride! It combines the jumps and tricks of freestyle with the excitement of mountain biking.

RACING:

BMX racing today is held at regional and national levels. It's a great way to meet cool friends that have the same interests as you.

Brakes

Tires

Frame

Pedals

Pegs

Mat Hoffman

Mat Hoffman is the greatest vert-ramp rider in the history of the sport. He started in freestyle BMX as an amateur at the age of 13. At 16, he was the youngest pro in the sport ever. He has numerous world records and has invented more than 100 tricks like the 900; Flip faki (backflip which includes landing backwards); and Flair (backflip with a 180 degree turn). The Hoffman Sports Association (H.S.A.) organizes Freestyle BMX events worldwide, including ESPN's X Games and all international X Games bicycle stunt events. Mat has been injured a number of times and has had 15 operations. Mat is also vice president of the International BMX Freestyle Federation and the United States BMX Freestyle Federation.

History

In 1938, Schwinn brought out the "Fore-wheel" brake, "Cantilever Frame" and the "Spring Fork" resulting in the ancestor of today's mountain bike. The specialized Stumpjumper mountain bike was mass-produced in the U.S. inspired by bikes produced by California icons Gary Fisher, Joe Breeze, and Tom Richey. Then in 1987 the full suspension bike with front and rear shocks was introduced. This revolutionized the sport of mountain biking.

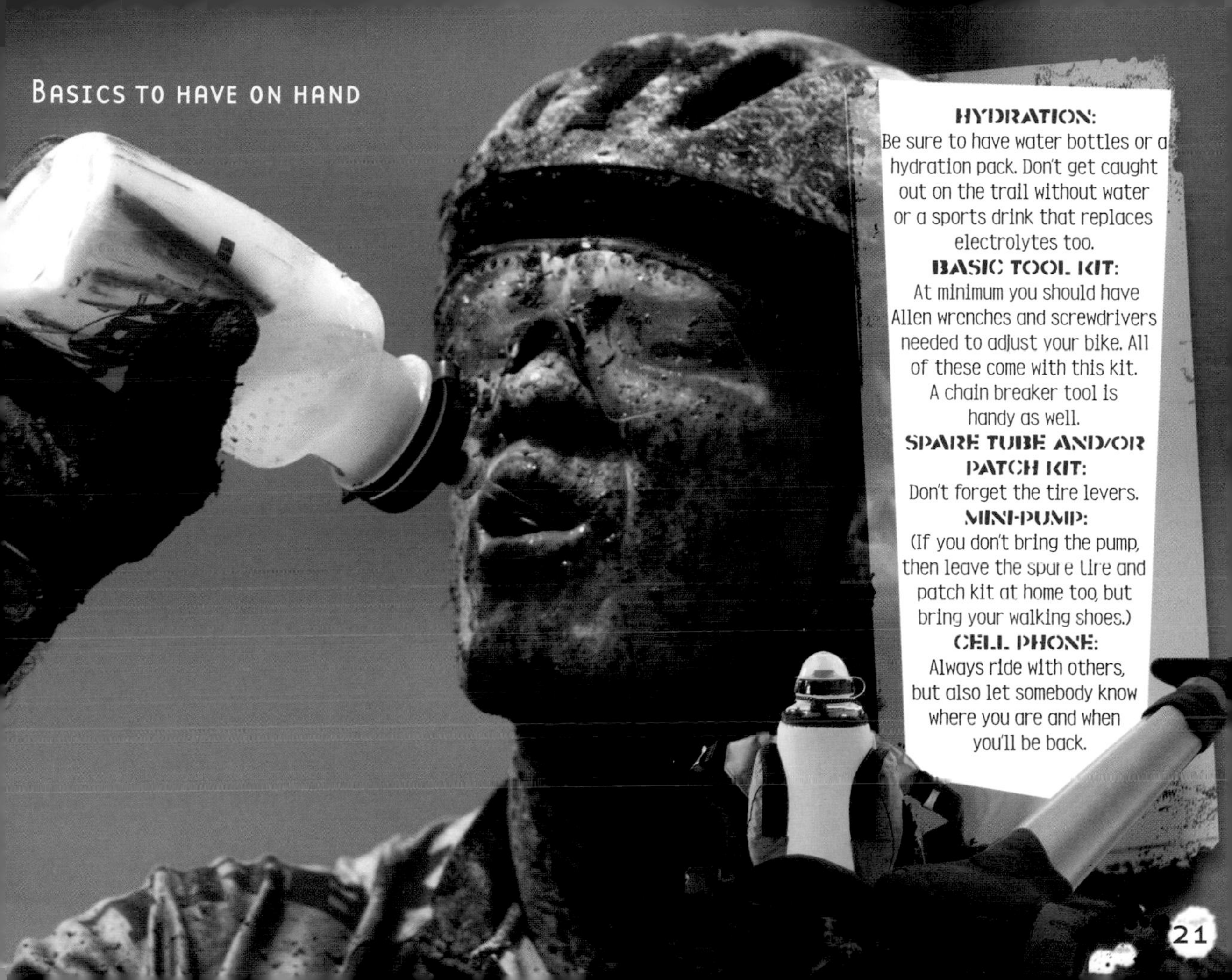

Basics to have on hand

HYDRATION:
Be sure to have water bottles or a hydration pack. Don't get caught out on the trail without water or a sports drink that replaces electrolytes too.

BASIC TOOL KIT:
At minimum you should have Allen wrenches and screwdrivers needed to adjust your bike. All of these come with this kit. A chain breaker tool is handy as well.

SPARE TUBE AND/OR PATCH KIT:
Don't forget the tire levers.

MINI-PUMP:
(If you don't bring the pump, then leave the spare tire and patch kit at home too, but bring your walking shoes.)

CELL PHONE:
Always ride with others, but also let somebody know where you are and when you'll be back.

Susan Haywood

Susan Haywood has been riding her mountain bike since the early 90s. Her first major win in the pros came in the 2003 NORBA National Championship Series in Big Bear, CA. Susan has one numerous first and second place finishes. She never dreamed she could make a living as a pro mountain biker.

GET OUT THERE!

Taking a variety of trails is a good way to build skills, confidence, and endurance. You'll need a lot of all of these to master the back roads. There are mountain bike trails throughout the U.S., Canada, and Europe. See if you have a mountain biking club in your area. Sometimes you can find them listed on the Internet. Ultimately, mountain bike riding is about having fun. Don't get caught up in the proper way to ride your bike or a certain style. If you're riding your bike and having fun, then you've got it figured out.

uidelines of the trail

1. Have fun. Sounds simple, right? But it's tough when you're falling down and scraping your body.
2. Never stop in the middle of the trail. If you have to stop, pull off to the side and provide a clear path for others.
3. Keep the trails in good shape. They are maintained by volunteers. Skidding your back tire was cool when you were 7, but it's not cool on that sweet descent.
4. Always stay on the trail. Sounds pretty simple, but it's more than important. We're not talking about when you lose control of your bike and take a nosedive into the bushes. We're talking about not creating shortcuts or straightening the trail.
5. Only ride on dry trails. Nothing damages a trail more than riding in knee-deep mud and rain. It's safest to wait 24 hours after a good rain for a trail to dry out.
6. Always yield to hikers. It's the neighborly thing to do. You should also yield to horses. It's not a bad idea to say something, so the horse is aware you're there.
7. Be an ambassador of the sport. This can be as simple as saying hello to passing riders or driving responsibly. Slow down and show some respect.

Tricking it out

STICKERS –

There are a bunch of stickers that come with this kit, or you can get them from all kinds of different stores.

REFLECTORS –

You can go all out and put reflectors all over your bike. You won't be missed for sure!

LIGHTS –

Bring on the lights! There are these really cool lights that screw right on to the tire stem. They are motion sensor lights, so while you're riding it looks like there is a streak of light going through your spokes.

PEGS –

Some BMX bikes come with pegs, but if you want to add them, it's easy! They screw right onto the bolt on the front and back tire. Pegs are used for doing flatland and vert tricks.

BIKE SPINNERS –

The spinners attach to the front and rear wheel of most bikes. Check with the manufacturer to make sure that particular spinner will fit your bike. If you can handle a screwdriver and a wrench, you can install spinners.

You can always change out seats, handle bars, and tires. If the seat doesn't feel comfortable...then you need a more comfortable place to sit, my friend.

So many tires, so little time!

Clincher Tires - Conventional bicycle tires. They consist of an outer tire and a separate tube. The edges of the tire hook over the edges of the rim, and air pressure holds everything in place. These are very easy to replace if you get a flat.

Tubular Tires - Totally Tubular! The two edges of this tire are sewn together around the inner tube. Everything is glued onto special rims. You'll find these in most high-performance bicycles. But, if they are not installed correctly, a serious crash can result.

Front Tire	Rear Tire	Uses
Smooth, no tread or fine pattern	Smooth, no tread or fine pattern	Great on pavement
Wider tire, knobby treads	Wider tire, knobby treads	Off-road only
Knobby tread, smooth center	Knobby tread, smooth center	Good on dirt, ok on pavement
Narrower	Wider	If carrying a heavy weight in back
Wider	Narrower	Better cornering, comfortable ride, and shock absorption
Aggressive tread	Smooth	Front wheel traction for soft conditions, like sand or mud, great for BMX racing, good for combination riding (half pavement, half off-road)

Tires Made Easy

Tools of the trade

You need to carry a basic tool kit with you when you ride. The tool that comes with this kit has a lot of the basics including allen wrenches, hub wrenches, and a couple of screw drivers. You may also like to get a chain remover to fix a broken chain or chain problems on the road. A tire tube patch is a must have in case you blow a tire.

CHAIN REMOVER

PATCH KIT

YOUR TOOL

Tune Your Ride

Chain maintenance

LUBE IT!

Keeping your chain lubricated is the best way to keep it lasting a long time. Put a drip of lubricant on every pin to keep your chain happy. Yes, this can get messy, but it is the best way to lube the entire chain. Let the chain soak up the lube for about 15 to 20 minutes. Then, wipe it dry with a clean rag. This will keep your chain from attracting all that nasty dirt.

CLEAN IT!

A good old-fashioned cleaning is a great idea for your chain if you've been riding in foul weather, gone through some mud, sand, or road debris. Flip your bike onto its seat and handlebars on a clean towel. Get some dish soap. Put a dollop (about a quarter size circle) of dish soap in the center of a sponge or rag. Remove the grease, grime, and old lube by placing the rag on and slightly around the chain. Turn your pedals backward (slowly) until the entire chain is clean. Rinse the rag and repeat until the chain doesn't give you a smudge on the rag. Leave the chain on the bike while cleaning it to prevent the chain from getting weak.

KINKS

While you're doing your chain's bi-monthly maintenance, check for tight links. To do this, back pedal slowly and watch the chain. If it jumps or jerks, there is a tight link. First try flexing it from five links up to loosen it. If it doesn't loosen, get a new chain.

No one likes to get a flat, but they do happen! Flats can be caused by heat, damage, worn equipment, and other problems with the tires, or even the road. Get over it and fix it!

REMOVING THE TIRE

Squeeze the tire to make sure all the air is out of the inner tube before you remove the tire from the rim. Use your thumbs to push the tire away from the rim. Use a tire lever to pop the tire off one side of the rim and expose the inner tube.

REPAIR THE TUBE

Fill the inner tube with a little bit of air. Turn the tube around, near your ear and listen for a hissing sound. That's air escaping. If you still can't find the hole, slowly turn the tube in a pot of water until you see bubbles. Good job! You found the leak. Get your patch kit out. Read the instructions. Patch the hole, and you're good to go!

UH OH!

Your patch kit didn't work? Well, I'm sorry my friend, you'll have to go get a new inner tube. Also, if you used a patch to get yourself home, you should really replace the inner tube and the patch kit soon, so you don't have a repeat of walking home with a flat tire!

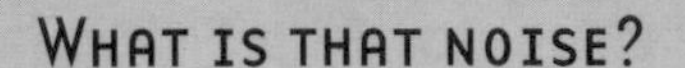

WHAT IS THAT NOISE?

Pop! Tap, Tap! Creak! Grind! Crunch! What in the world is all that noise coming from your bike?

LOOSE CRANKS –

Remove the dust caps and tighten the crank bolt with a socket or allen wrench (It will depend on your bike). If that doesn't work, you'll need to clean the spindle and the hole in the crank.

LOOSE CHAINRINGS –

Check the bolts that hold the chainrings to the crank spider and tighten any loose ones.

CRUNCH!
CREAK!

OTHER COMMON PROBLEMS

BOTTOM BRACKET–

Oh, what a racket if water gets into the bearings! Be sure to get those bearings repacked once in a while.

NOISY WHEELS–

First, check your spokes. They come loose all the time. Look for spokes that have pulled through the rims. Uh oh! It's time to get a new rim. Also, take the wheel to a bike shop to have it balanced or trued, to use the correct term. Sometimes those little pesky spokes will make a clicking noise where they cross over one another. Try a little lube at the crossing. Check for any junk stuck to the tire, like glass, rocks, nails...you name it!

LOOSE SEAT–

Is your seat clicking? Tighten the seat post. A good old allen wrench should do the trick.

NOISY FORK-

Oooo, not so good! If it's a stiff fork, it shouldn't be making noise. If it is, take it to a bike shop for an inspection.

NOISY STEM OR HANDLEBARS-

Make sure the handlebars are secure in the stem. Tighten with an allen wrench if you need to. If all else fails, take the stem out and clean it.

CHAIN-

Hey, we've already talked about that! Keep it clean and lubed and it shouldn't be making any noise! If it's loose, it's time to get a new chain (see page 27.)

THE SKATEBOARD

Where'd that thing come from?

In the 1940s, people started taking metal skates apart and attaching them to wood planks. The 1950s brought about the term "sidewalk surfing". Surfers took their boards and attached skates to them as a way of getting around. Early skateboards looked like mini surfboards with no kicktail, and narrow trucks with clay wheels. Kicktails came along in 1967. This gave the skateboarder tighter turning, braking, and of course more trick ability. With the advent of urethane wheels and precision bearings, skaters got superior grip and ride quality. This is about the time that pool riding, vert, freestyle, slalom, and pipe riding took off. Skateboarding has never looked back!

Tony Hawk

He may not skate competitively anymore, but he is one of the best-known names in the sport of skateboarding. Tony Hawk got on a board for the first time when he was nine years old. Before he started skateboarding he considered himself kind of a spaz. Tony Hawk turned pro at the age of 14 and began winning almost every skateboarding contest he entered. He has invented tons of tricks, including the first ever 900 (two and half turns in midair). Tony's house has special floors so he can skate inside the house! How cool is that?

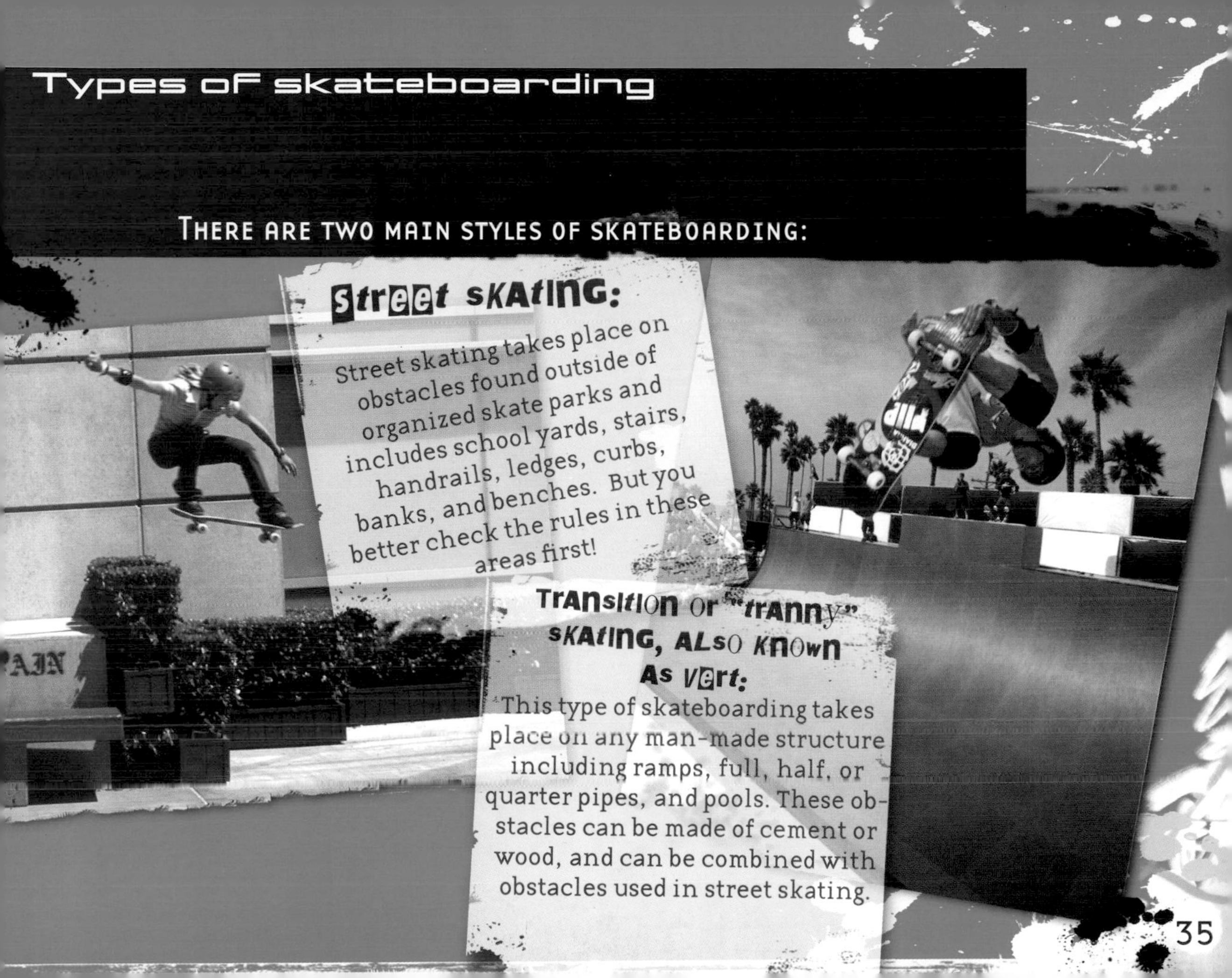

Types of skateboarding

THERE ARE TWO MAIN STYLES OF SKATEBOARDING:

Street skating:

Street skating takes place on obstacles found outside of organized skate parks and includes school yards, stairs, handrails, ledges, curbs, banks, and benches. But you better check the rules in these areas first!

Transition or "tranny" skating, also known as vert:

This type of skateboarding takes place on any man-made structure including ramps, full, half, or quarter pipes, and pools. These obstacles can be made of cement or wood, and can be combined with obstacles used in street skating.

NATURAL OR GOOFY?

What style do you skate? A natural skater has his left foot on the front of the board, but a goofy skater has his right foot on the front of the board. No, that doesn't mean you ARE goofy, it's just the term. Put whichever foot feels better on the front of the board.

NATURAL

GOOFY

Bucky Lasek

He's the vert champ of the X Games. Getting big air has been no problem for pro skater, Bucky Lasek, who has been skateboarding since he was 13. He entered the world of professional skateboarding in the 90s. He's won several gold medals in the vert event at the X Games. He is considered one of the world's most creative skaters. He skates three to four hours everyday and has invented many new tricks.

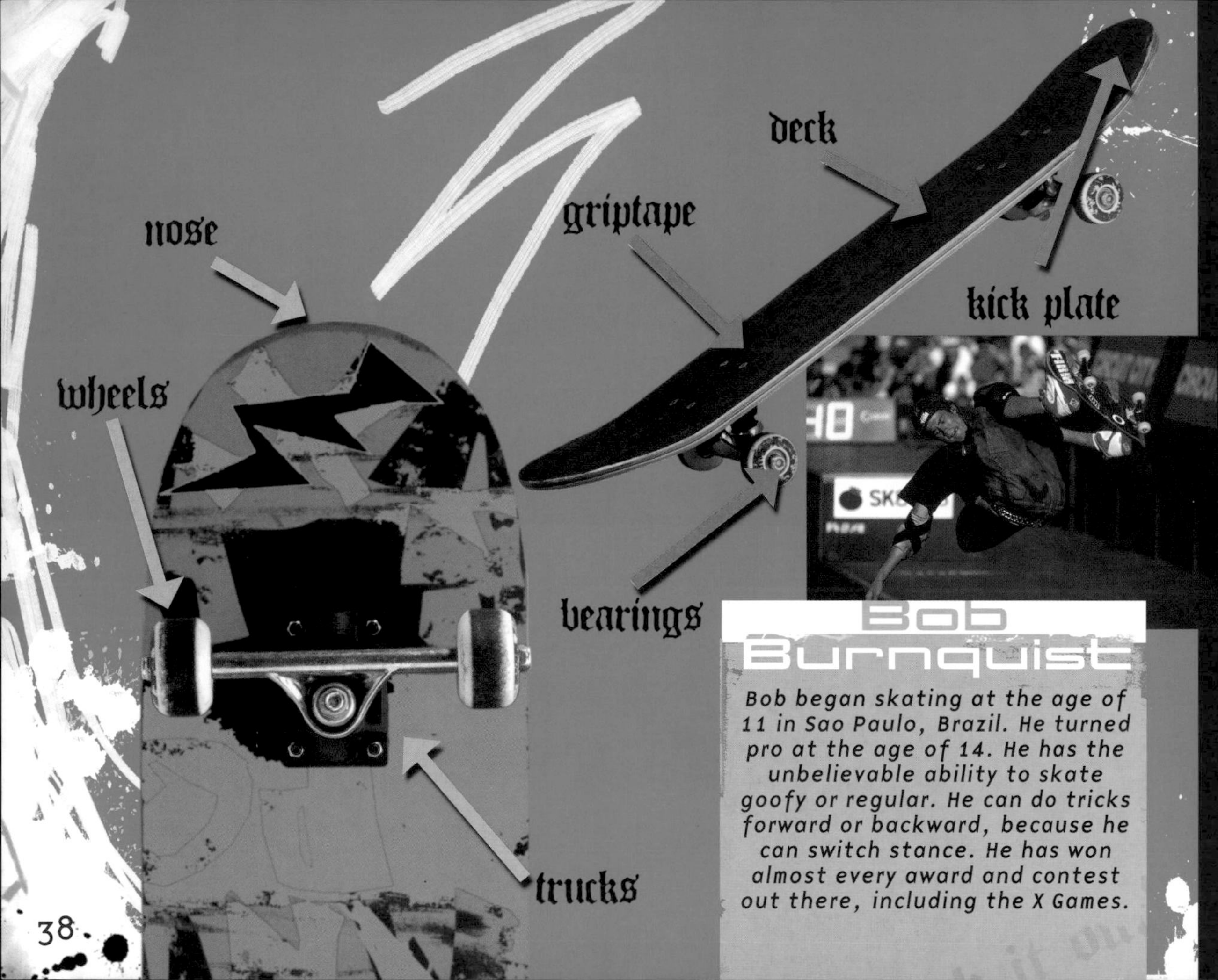

Bob Burnquist

Bob began skating at the age of 11 in Sao Paulo, Brazil. He turned pro at the age of 14. He has the unbelievable ability to skate goofy or regular. He can do tricks forward or backward, because he can switch stance. He has won almost every award and contest out there, including the X Games.

Ready to rip it?

If your parents are tired of hearing, "Must have skateboard! Must have skateboard," then you have been sucked into the skateboarding vortex. Alright rookie, let's take a look at what you need.

BUYING SKATEBOARD GEAR CAN BE OVERWHELMING! SO HERE'S A FEW TIPS FOR NEWBIES:

1. Choose the best board you can afford. Cheaper skateboards are not made to quality standards and can be dangerous.

2. Today's skateboards are made of six or seven layers of maple plywood.
Street boards are usually 29 inches.
Stunt and freestyle boards are 27 inches.
Vert and downhill boards are usually 30 inches.

3. Deck curves: A semi-flat board gives you a comfortable feel, but the lack of curve makes them a little weaker. A board with more drastic concave curves may feel strange, but the board is strong and allows for radical tricks.

4. Wheels: The wheels come in 50mm to 60mm (measured on the outside diameter). They work the same way as the decks size. The smaller wheel is better for street, and the bigger wheels are better for vert and downhill. But, it does come down to your preference.

5. Trucks: There really isn't a lot of difference between trucks. Make sure the truck axels are not longer than the width of the board. That's about it!

6. Bearings: These are the only product in skateboarding where price plays a role. Pretty much, you get what you pay for.

7. Riser Pads: These little guys serve a couple of purposes, but both are optional. There are two kinds, soft and hard. They come in $\frac{1}{8}$, $\frac{1}{4}$, or $\frac{3}{8}$- inch thickness. The soft pads lessen vibration (not enough that you'll notice, but enough that the nuts and bolts won't rattle loose). The hard ones keep bigger wheels from scraping against the deck on sharp turns. Depending on how tight or loose you like your trucks, you won't need risers with wheels smaller than 55mm.

If you're still not sure about what to get, check out your local skateboarding shop, or some of the shops online. They'll be a great help!

SAFETY FIRST! THIS IS NOT AN OPTION!

Skateboarding is physically demanding and mentally challenging, but it can be dangerous. Take the time to learn proper skills and definitely follow safety precautions.

Ride only to your own abilities, not those of your friends.

Develop your skills starting with the basics, that means learning how to ride comfortably, turn, and stop on your skateboard.

Choose a quality board, like we talked about on page 33.

You'll need a helmet that is CPSC approved.

Elbow and knee pads, wrist guards, and gloves may be needed too. These will protect you from serious injuries and road rashes.

The safety gear you use will depend on the style of skating you do. If you are riding vert or bowls, you'll need to wear all your safety gear due to the speed and the heights of your big air. Street riders go at low speeds, so they tend to wear less gear, but helmets are still a must.

DO NOT SKATE IN WET WEATHER.
You'll end up ruining your bearings and your wheels will lock up. I bet you can imagine the damage to you that will result.

TRY NOT TO SKATE THROUGH MUD, SAND, OR GRAVEL.
Even if you could, it's the fastest way to ruin your wheels.

MAKE SURE YOU KEEP YOUR BOLTS TIGHT,
but not overly tight.

Persuading your Parentals!

I'll wear the body armor, I mean protective gear all the time! See page 40.

Skateboarding can be done anywhere there is a smooth, traffic free pavement. However, I'll check the laws in the area. I won't skate in places that do not allow skateboarding. I'll do the right thing!

Skateboarding is one of the safest sports for youths. According to the National Safety Coun-cil and the Consumer Safety Commission, there are 6,200,000 skateboarders with 27,718 injuries per year. When you compare that to football with 14,700,000 players with 409,296 injuries, that's not too shabby.

The best part about skateboarding is that the maintenance is relatively low compared with other sports. You also need only a few tools. The ones in this kit will do you just fine.

thE dECK

Skateboarding is tough on boards. And they do wear out with a lot of riding. So, it will have to be replaced. If your board is badly cracked, get a new deck. Don't risk getting hurt.

tRuCK hARDWARE

This one is easy! Normal riding will cause the hardware on the trucks to loosen from the deck. Use a screwdriver or allen wrench (depends on your board) to tighten the hardware.

gRIP

The grip tape on your board can be cleaned with a plastic bristle brush and some warm water. Unfortunately, it cannot be removed, so don't even try. Don't get the board soaked. The deck will split and the grip tape will pull-up if the deck gets too wet. Use a semi-clean towel (and not your Mom's good ones!) to dry the board some more. Then let it dry completely in the sun.

Trucks

If the rubber bushings are all smashed, it's time to replace them. Replacing them can make your trucks ride like new again. To do this, remove the kingpin tension nut, work the old cushion off, replace the metal retainer cup, and put the new cushion on. Check the whole truck for cracks, and replace them if necessary.

ADJUSTING THE TRUCKS: As soon as you get your board, get out the wrench that fits your skateboard. Remember, righty tighty, lefty loosey. Here's how you test it. Put your board on a flat surface. Put one foot on the deck. Put all your weight on the near side of the board until it reaches its max lean. Quickly remove your foot and the board should snap back to center. If the trucks feel unstable or lean too much, tighten them. If they feel too stiff, loosen them up a few turns. For riding on small hills and flats, the board should be 1 to 2 inches from the ground. For flat riding, it should be about 1 inch from the ground. For steep hills or ramps, your board should barely move when you put weight on it.

Bearings

The little metal pieces that allow the wheel to spin are called the bearings. If your wheels don't spin freely, the bearings may need to be cleaned or replaced. If the wheels make a little noise or are rough, you'll need to clean them. However, some bearings are not made to take apart. It would be a good idea to take your board in for service at this point.

Wheels

Check your wheels often. They should not have any damage, flat spots, or chunks of urethane missing. If they do, replace them.

Axle Wheel Lock Nuts

These hold your wheels to the trucks. ALWAYS check these before you start skateboarding. Axle nuts wear out and loosen with tightening and removal. If you even think there is a problem with them, get them replaced. There is nothing like losing a wheel in the middle of some big air.

STICKERS –
Some skaters are purists and don't put any stickers on their board unless they are directly sponsored by that particular company. This is a matter of personal preference! So, if you want to add stickers to your board, they're in your kit. Definitely put them on the bottom of the board, so they do not interfere with the grip tape.

WHEELS –
The word on the street says it is cool to replace your wheels with...are you ready...speed skate wheels. You get a lot more control and grab on the pavement. Now you can also change out the wheels for your favorite color.

SPINNERS –
They look very cool! If you are really into skateboarding tricks, this will throw your balance off, so be careful! Wheel stickers might be a better alternative. Check out what's in your kit.

Bam Magera

Viva La Bam!
Goofy rider, Bam Magera (pronounced ma-jer-a), has been described as "a skate guru who's skidded face-first down the vert ramp one too many times." He has a popular series on MTV where he performs outrageous and dangerous stunts for the camera. Bam has directed or acted in several movies and TV shows.

OLLIE

Make sure you always wear a helmet!

In 2004, Alan Gelfand was officially credited with the invention of the skateboard trick the "Ollie." He invented the trick in 1976 when he was only 13 years old.

To do an ollie, press the foot down on the tail of the board to push the deck off the ground. With both feet on the board, lift the heel of your back foot so your weight is on the ball of your foot and your toes, and is centered on the tip of the tail. Your front foot should be about ⅔ up the board, angled slightly forward. Smack the tail to the ground with your back foot and jump off of your back foot. As you jump, your front foot slides up to the nose, pulling the board into the air. While in the air, level out your board and wait for the landing. Always land with your knees bent.

MANUAL

Elissa Steamer

Skater-girl! Elissa Steamer is by far the best female skater in the history of skateboarding. Elissa holds her own with the boys and has since1989 when she started skateboarding. She went pro in 1998 and promptly won the women's street competition in the Slam City Jam in Vancouver, British Colombia. She regularly makes the cut, even among the male competitors. Elissa has won many firsts in her career and continues to define the role of women in this male-dominated sport.

If you want to improve balance, and have something else to do while you're skating, a manual is the way to go. Put your back foot on the tail, but very close if not covering the rear-ing mounting bolts. Your front foot should be around the front mounting trucks. The wide stance will give you the control you need with your front and back feet. Roll with the front wheels off the ground.

POP SHOVIT

Start into an ollie, except rotate your body inward. Then, kick your back foot behind you and your board will rotate inward. Keep your shoulders and body straight. As the board starts moving up, then jump up with the board. The harder you pop the board, the higher your board will go. You've got to land it to finish the trick!

360 FLIP

This trick is a little more complicated than the kick flip, or Ollie. First, bend your knees. Then, have your front foot on the outer left side of the board. When you are in the air, instead of kicking the right part of the nose, kick the left part of the nose, which will cause it to spin the other way. Then, land with your feet back onto the board.

THE SKATE

A little background

The first roller skate came from a Belgian inventor named Joseph Merlin in 1760. However, in 1863 James Plimpton invented a skate that allowed people to skate around turns. After WWII, skating rinks started popping up all over. It has since become a popular pastime for everyone. Two brothers who wanted to train for hockey in the summertime redesigned inlines skates in the late 80s. Now, inline skating became one of the most popular sports in America. Now, extreme inline takes its cue from skateboarding. You'll see inline skaters doing many of the same tricks that skateboarders have been doing for years.

Use Your Head!

Are you ready to be a hardcore skater, safety first...

WRIST GUARDS –
This is a plastic splint that supports the wrist if you fall on it. It is a must-have for safety.

ELBOW AND KNEE PADS –
These will save your elbows and knees from road rash. You must wear them if you are going to ride vert or play inline hockey.

HELMET –
Don't leave home without it.

CLOTHES –
Yes, you want your clothes to look cool, but they need to protect your body too. Wear loose fitting and light clothes for most types of inline skating, but if you're going to do inline hockey, you'll want a little more coverage.

NEVER SKATE IN TRAFFIC OR ON PRIVATE PROPERTY. CHECK THE LAWS IN YOUR AREA. IF IT SAYS NO SKATEBOARDING, THIS APPLIES TO YOU TOO.

DO NOT SKATE IN THE DARK.

Pieces and parts

Get the best skates your money can buy. These are the things that are going to have you cruisin' and stylin'.

Skate types:

Aggressive Skates –

These skates have it all, but they are not for the weak of heart. These babies have small, hard wheels, a hard shell, a lace or buckle that doesn't stick out, a removable liner, and no brake!

Rec. Skates –

These are the recreational variety of skates. This is a brake at the back of the skate and big wheels.

Speed Skates –

These skates have five very hard wheels, making for a longer blade. The boot is lightweight.

Hockey Skates –

These look just like ice skates with wheels. There are no clips or buckles, only laces.

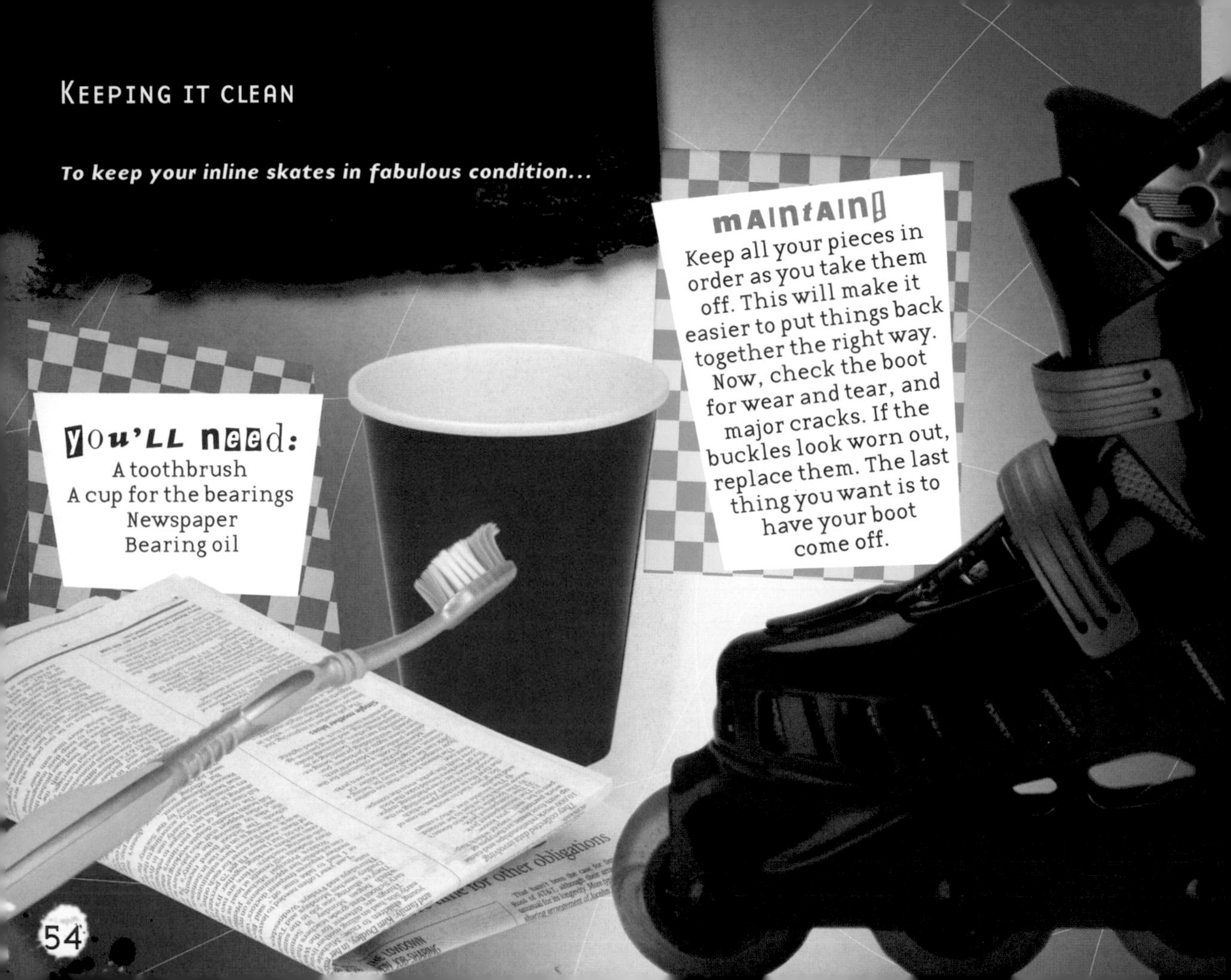

Keeping it clean

To keep your inline skates in fabulous condition...

You'll need:

A toothbrush
A cup for the bearings
Newspaper
Bearing oil

Maintain

Keep all your pieces in order as you take them off. This will make it easier to put things back together the right way. Now, check the boot for wear and tear, and major cracks. If the buckles look worn out, replace them. The last thing you want is to have your boot come off.

Rotating the wheels:

Ok, now for the hassle of rotating the wheels. It's a pain, but it needs to be done. It will make your wheels last much longer. First, undo all the wheel bolts. Take a look at the illustration to see how to rotate them. While the wheels are off, clean them, pop out the bearings and if needed, clean them too. Use a toothbrush to get all the dirt and junk off the wheels and the bearings. Let everything dry. Then, add a few drops of lube to each bearing.

Here's A Few Quick tips:

- **Don't skate through water. It will rust your bearings.**
- **Don't skate through mud, gravel, or sand. It will get into the bearings, and they will have to be replaced.**
- **Tighten the wheel bolts, but don't over tighten.**
- **Make sure you secure the buckles everytime you skate. It will save you unnecessary road rash.**

Trick out your inlines!

Here are just a few ideas:

Wheel upgrades – Wheels wear out! It's a fact of life. But here is the perfect opportunity to choose new ones that will better meet your skating needs (speed, maneuverability, and handling). Again, check with your skate shop for more advice.

GRIND!

PUNK PUNK

Custom Fitted Boot– If you get blisters or discomfort from your skates, there are pads and inserts that will help. Check with your local skate shop to find an experienced custom boot fitter.

Stickers – You have a bunch in your kit to choose from.

Kite skating

Kite skating originated in the 90s, when rollerbladers used parafoil kites to propel them across parking lots, dry lake beds, grassy fields, and sandy beaches. The craze really took off with the advent of the off-road inline skates called the Wheels of Doom or Kite Skates. They were made from a pair of inline boots with the wheels removed. The boots are then fitted with scooter wheels. Now kite skaters are sailing along with all the wind power they can find. They can reach speeds of55+ mph.

What ever happened to the roller skate or Speed skates 101

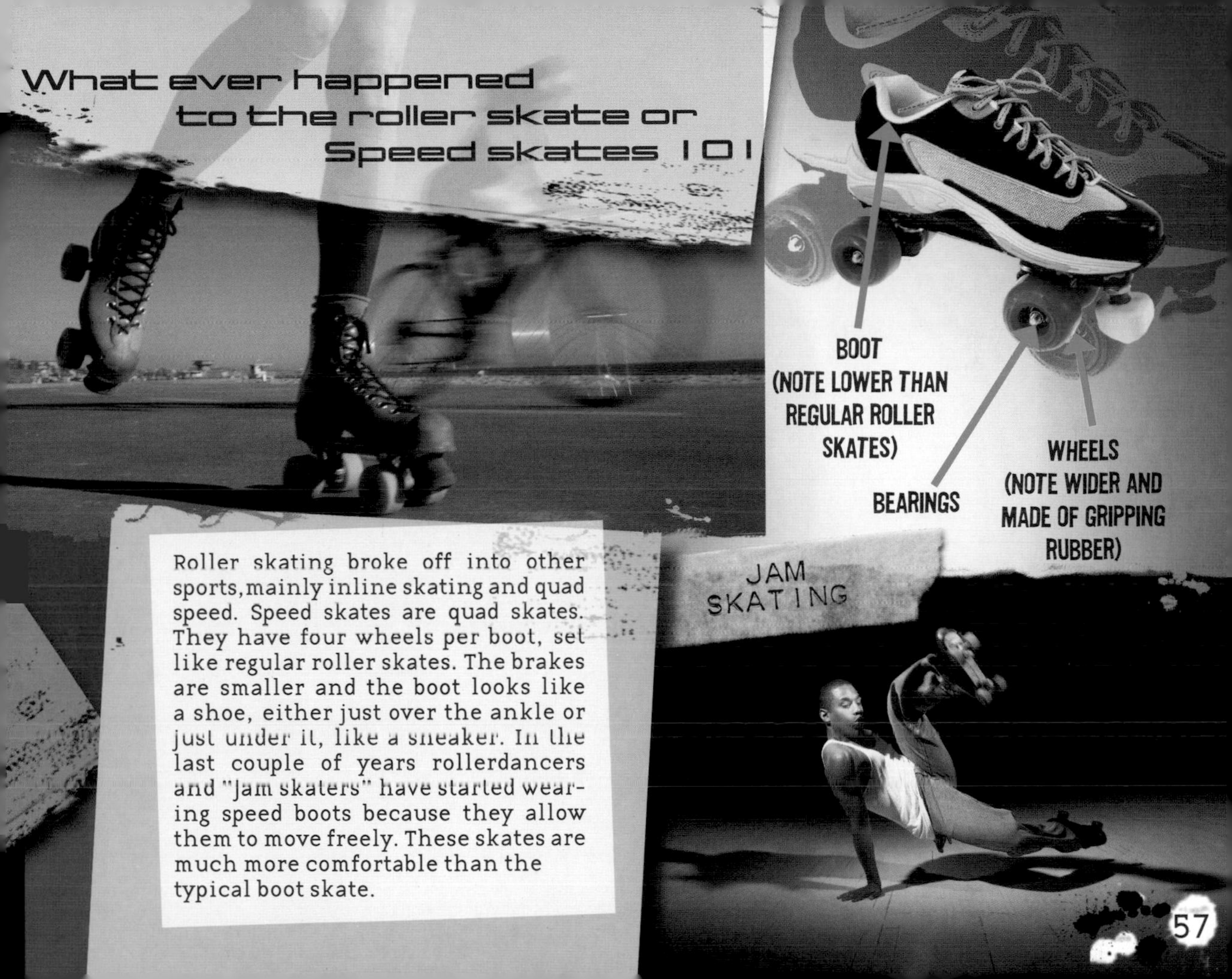

Roller skating broke off into other sports, mainly inline skating and quad speed. Speed skates are quad skates. They have four wheels per boot, set like regular roller skates. The brakes are smaller and the boot looks like a shoe, either just over the ankle or just under it, like a sneaker. In the last couple of years rollerdancers and "Jam skaters" have started wearing speed boots because they allow them to move freely. These skates are much more comfortable than the typical boot skate.

Keeping it clean

Keeping your speed skates in tip-top condition is similar to the maintenance routine for inline skates.

THESE ARE INLINE SPEED SKATES.

...ne Your Ride

Here Are A Few things to Keep in Mind:

1. *If wheels are not tight, tighten with an allen wrench.*

2. *If wheels move from side-to-side, replace the bearing system.*

3. *If wheels do not move freely, clean your bearing system.*

4. *Replace wheels when they are worn.*

Trick out your speed skates!

Quad skates can be tricked out just as easily as inlines.

There are tons of stickers you can use to jazz up your ride. Or use colorful permanent marker for an individualized look.

You can even change out the wheels for speed and maneuverability.

Loosen the trucks slightly for better turning.

Mountain skates

There is another type of quad skate that is beginning to take off. The all terrain or "Mountain Skate" has wide trucks and very large tractor style wheels (about 4 inches in diameter). They are used for skating over just about anything that is in your path. Mike Vail designed these new quad skates and is one of the few practitioners of this sport. They can tear up trails, grass, gravel, dirt, concrete, and more. These skates are appropriate for flat or downhill terrain. Now that's rad!

Heelys are the latest craze in skating. They are a pair shoes that come with a single removable wheel in each heel. You can walk and then shift your weight and you're rollin'! Some Heelys even come with a grind plate to slide down a railing. Oh yeah, that's called a grind.

WhEEL

shOE

Here's how to start:

1. Lift the ball of your foot and find your center of balance. You can do this with one foot at a time to start.
2. Start with your feet together.
3. Step forward with your stronger leg and balance on the heel.
4. While the strong leg is balanced, push off with the trailing leg and quickly lift the ball of that foot to a balancing position on the wheel.
5. Pull yourself along a rail until you find your center of balance.
6. Keep the trailing leg directly behind your strong leg as if your toes on the back foot are superglued to the front heel, toes up!

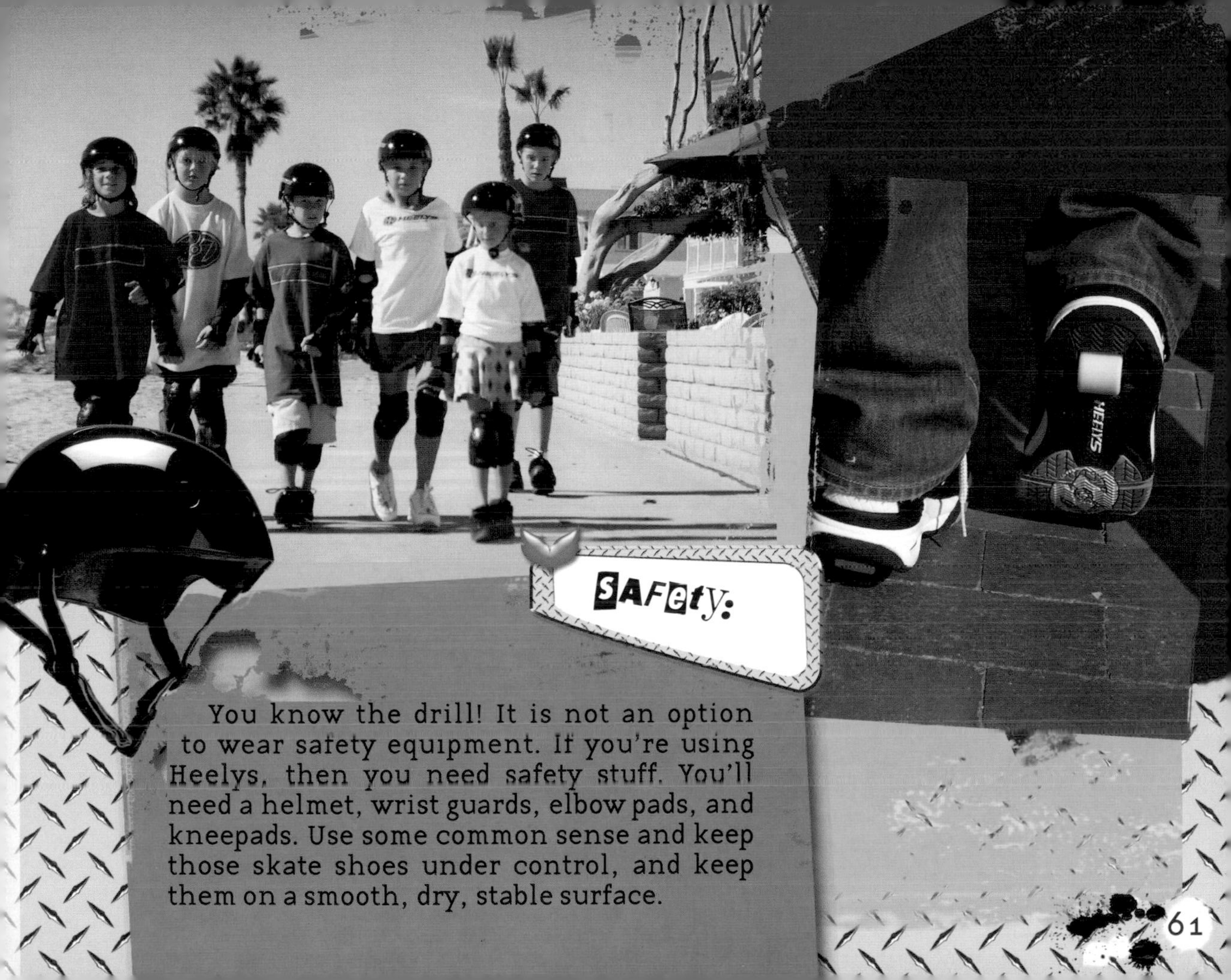

SAFETY:

You know the drill! It is not an option to wear safety equipment. If you're using Heelys, then you need safety stuff. You'll need a helmet, wrist guards, elbow pads, and kneepads. Use some common sense and keep those skate shoes under control, and keep them on a smooth, dry, stable surface.

GLOSSARY OF TERMS

360 Flip - A 360 degree backside, varial, kickflip.
Air - Riding a skateboard, bike, or skates into the air, land it, and continue on.
Babyheads - roundish rocks found in a loose pile on hairpin turns or other difficult sections of a trail. death cookies are smaller.
Backside - Turns or rotations in the direction your toes point, so that your back is facing the outside of the arc. (Sometimes abbreviated as "bs" or "b/s")
Bail - An intentional fall from a bike, skateboard, or skates to avoid serious injury.
BMX - Bicycle motocross, an off-road race over a prepared obstacle course. BMX is a type of bicycle.
Brake levers - the levers mounted to each side of the handlebars that you pull with your fingers to apply the brakes.
Bunny hop - to lift both bike wheels off the ground by crouching down and then exploding upward, pulling the bike with you.
Cable guide or housing - A tube, mounted on the frame, that guides the brake or shift cable.
Caliper brakes - Brakes with a pair of brake pads on opposite sides of the wheel rim.
Cantilever brakes - Caliper brakes that are below the rim and attached to the frame or fork.
Chainline - The path the chain takes between front and rear sprockets.
Chainrings — the front sprockets on any bike that the chain goes around.
Chain skip — when a chain slips off the sprocket teeth when pedaling hard.
Chain tool - A tool for disconnecting a chain link.
Clincher tire, Wired-on tire - A tire that stays on the rim by a small lip that gets caught between the rim walls.
Coaster brake - A brake built into the rear that works by pedaling backwards.
Cranks - the arms that transfer your pedaling to the chain, which turns the wheels.
Deck - The laminated surface of a skateboard.
Derailleur - The assembly that "derails" the chain from one sprocket to another, in order to change gears.

Domestique – a rider who supports the team leader.
Endo - the maneuver of flying unexpectedly over the handlebars.
Etape – a race stage.
Fork - the front wheel attaches to the fork. It rotates the front wheel when you steer.
Frame - the core of the bike.
Full suspension - a mountain bike with both front and rear suspension.
Goofy-foot - Someone whose normal skate stance is with the right foot forward.
Grind – any skateboarding trick where you move along the edge of an object with your trucks, scraping (or grinding) the object.
Grips - the rubber pieces where you place your hands on the handlebars of a bike.
Grip Shifter - A shifter where the gear is changed by twisting the grip.
Grip Tape - The sandpaper-like tape with an adhesive back placed on the skateboard to provide a non-slip surface
Helmet – piece of equipment used to protect your head, must be worn for skating, skateboarding, and cycling. Also called Brain Bucket.
Hybrid - A bicycle with characteristics of both road and mountain bikes.
Jet - to accelerate quickly and go very fast.
Kickflip – Ollie, then the front foot goes toward the heel side of the board, flicking the board with your toes, board flips, and you land.
Kicktail – the tail of the skateboard.
Lubricant - keeps your bearings rolling quickly, quietly, and smoothly.
Manual - Balancing while riding a skateboard on two wheels.
Nose - The front end of the board, from the front two truck bolts to the tip of the deck.
Ollie - The basis for most skateboarding tricks. The back foot smacks the tail of the board against the ground while the front foot pulls the board up into the air.
Patron – the winner of the race from the previous year.
Peloton – the large main group of riders.
Poser - Pretender; someone that dresses like a skateboarder but doesn't skateboard.
Powerslide - a two-wheel sideways slide, with the foot opposite the direction of travel.

Regular-foot - a normal skate stance with the left foot forward, also called natural.
Rigid - a bike with no suspension.
Rim - The outer part of a bicycle wheel that supports the tube and the tire.
Road Bike - A bicycle designed for riding on the road.
Road rash – An skin scrape caused by a crash on pavement.
Saddle - A bicycle seat.
Shifters - the little dial or lever mounted to the handlebars, next to the grips, that you use to shift gears.
Slam - A bad, unexpected fall.
Sprocket - One of the toothed wheels that mesh with the chain to transfer power from the cranks to the drivewheel.
Stage race - A race in which a different course is gone over each day. The winner is the racer with the lowest total time.
Suspension fork - A fork with shock absorber(s).
Switch-stance – Being able to switch from regular stance to goofy stance and skating as well both ways.
Tail - The back part of the skateboard, from the back two truck bolts, to the tip of the deck, also known as the kicktail.
Tight - Cool, rad, sick, sweet.
Tour De France - The most famous bicycle race in the world. It covers a thousand difficult, mountainous miles and extends over a three week period.
Tricked out - when a bike, skateboard, or skate has the latest and hottest components.
Trucks - The two parts of the skateboard connecting the deck with the wheels.
Truing a wheel - The process of making a wheel round by adjusting spoke tension.
Vert – refers to the type of skateboarding done on a ramp.
Vert Ramp - A half-pipe where the steepest section of the ramp is straight up and down.
Wheelie - lifting the front wheel off the ground.
Wonky - not functioning properly.

CHECK IT OUT!